PERSIST PAST PAIN

HOW TO LIVE POWERFULLY AFTER TRAGEDY

BY MADI STILL

WITH DENISE PETTI

ISBN-13: 978-1-7320544-0-0

Persist Past Pain: How to Live Powerfully After Tragedy

First Edition

For Derick, DJ and Noah.
My heart. My world. My why.

Acknowledgments

First, I want to thank God for providing me with purpose and the gift of voice. In those dark nights when I thought grief would consume me, I was never alone. He was with me, carrying me through the pain. For that I am forever His servant.

Next, I want to thank my editor, brand manager, my very own PB to my jelly, the "brave" Denise Petti. She's more than the Head Honcho of Redfeather Communications. She is the person who gives voice to my ideas. I'm forever grateful for the day she picked up the phone and agreed to work with me.

To my family and closest friends, you know the length of the journey it took me to cross the bridge from pain to purpose. Thank you for being a rock in my life and for being there in my grief and now in my success.

To my mentors in life, thank you for helping me develop the courage to follow my dream and share my story. There were times this was not easy, but you reminded me that my story matters.

To Derick and DJ, you are my entire world. Every day you help me see the beauty within me just by allowing me to love you more. Everything I do is for you.

Finally, to my prince in Heaven, Noah. Thank you for choosing me to be your Mama for two days. Thank you for fighting for two days so I could feel what it felt like to love someone more than I could dream. Thank you for my purpose. Continue to watch over your little brother; he's pretty amazing.

Forward
By Denise Petti

Persist is a curious word. We typically hear it used in the context of something argumentative, like reasoning with a stubborn child or something unrelenting, like the weather. Kids wear us out with their persistence. Rain persists and we soon tire of the dismal hue of the sky. But persistence in the face of pain is something of a different definition. Persistence past pain, as my dear friend Madi Still writes in this book, not only defines us, it refines us.

Like you, I know something about pain. I know something about grief. I know something about loss and trauma. I know something about hoping it was all just a terrible dream. I know something about wishing it away, about wanting to go back in time, about wanting to change the wheel of fate, of wanting everything to be different and better or, at the very least, the way it used to be.

Yet, here we are. Our hearts beat and the world continues to rotate on its axis, despite the enormity of the trials we've faced and endured. My father was killed in an accidental factory explosion in 1996, and in the wake of my overwhelming grief, I simply couldn't fathom the world being content to go on without him. People went to school and to work. They still went to the gym, bought groceries, cooked dinner, listened to the radio and sang along. People laughed. How could that be?

Some pain feels so insurmountable, carved so deep into the canyons of your soul, you can't conceive of ever really feeling happy again, of really ever feeling anything again. A huge part of you dies with the pain and we even rationalize our desperate sadness and devastation, reasoning that it somehow honors what we've lost and justifies our feelings or behaviors. We wear our grief like a broken and bent badge of honor. Don't attempt to take it away from us either. It's our pain. We earned it. And we cling to it, a sort of twisted form of life support.

Until someone like Madi comes along and changes the name of the grief game. In her own, signature way, she gets our attention. She shows us that pain alone is not enough to define a life. Even more, she helps us embrace the idea that personal empowerment wields power over pain. The agony and defeat that was dealt us does not have the final say. In her powerfully relatable way, she validates and affirms our attachment to pain by encouraging us to walk straight toward it, not away from it. By guiding us to connecting with the pain of our past, by showing us how to find our way back to some semblance of daily structure, financial stability and self-care, she sets us down on a powerful trajectory, leading us through recovering a sense of strength that will ultimately help us define our passion and take us over the bridge to live in and on purpose.

When I first met Madi, it was over the phone. I knew she was a nutrition coach and really into exercise. What struck me was not how fit and healthy she was, although that did leave an impression all on its own. What truly struck me was how REAL she is. There's just something about a person who has been through the fire. I didn't even know, for a good long while, the depth of pain and grief she had endured. Over the past several years I have come to know this amazing individual personally and I can say, with utmost respect and reverence, that having her come into my life has helped me persist past my own pain and embrace the kind of potential I might not have otherwise realized.

Together we have created a powerful brand whose mission it is to serve others. People flock to Madi; they are attracted to her like water. They come to be the grateful recipients of her proprietary program called PREP: Powerfully Restoring and Empowering People. She does this through her website, on her blog, on her YouTube channel, social media profiles, webinars, workshops, special events and even sharing her story as a speaker on the TEDx stage. For my part, let me say what an honor and a privilege it has been to watch her and her brand emerge, and to be in her sidecar every mile along the way.

Madi encourages us to have the guts to grieve. She is the grantor of this incredible trust, and we, the grantees. We need only follow her lead, this woman who has been there, who watched her two-day old son die before her very eyes. She lays out a simple structure for recovery, one that helped her realize her son's death would inevitably come to serve, not only her, but countless of us willing to embrace the bigger, deeper meaning. Which is to say, in life, even pain and loss can be a gift, if we are brave enough to receive.

This journey is yours. With Madi as your guide, I feel confident you will persist through the pain of your past and come out on the other side of these six sessions feeling like a different person. You'll want to hug the people you love and tell them how proud you are of their successes, and even their failures. You'll wake up earlier, pray a lot more, laugh a little harder, exercise daily, eat mindfully and tell your money where to go. In short, you'll begin living as if your life depends on it... because it does.

Persist Past Pain

Using Pain as a Bridge to Discovering Your Purpose

It's February 28, 2018. I'm typing this introduction while staring absentmindedly out of my window. The sun is high as are the temperatures, an aberration for what should be a cold, winter's day. My fingers stroke the keys, but it's not my screen that my mind focuses on; it's the hospital NICU, a mere twenty minutes' drive, that harbors my darkest memory: the day my son died.

This book is not being written as just a "feel good" book. Not all moments in life "feel" good, but they are meant for your good. This book is to give you the steps to persist past pain and discover your purpose. I'm here for the believers. The ones who believe they've reached the end of their ropes and they are ready for so much more. I'm here for you.

February 28, 2008 could have been my end. I could have chosen to die that day. Maybe not physically, but metaphorically. I could have chosen to traverse through this life a zombie forever; simply existing until my end. Today, again on February 28th, my son has been reborn. He is my testimony. He gives me purpose. He gives me a beautiful story and the greatest gift I could have ever received: the power to change a life.

What will you do with this gift? If your plan is to read "another good book" and toss it to the side, then I beseech you to wait until you're ready. This book isn't only for highlighting and note-taking; it's for life-altering manifestation of your dream. It's for transformation. It's for you to see that finding power in your health, finances, and joy, is what helps you to persist past pain and find success.

For this book, you will need an open mind and you will need to be free of the story you tell yourself and how your past has determined who you are to this day. Our thoughts become feelings. Our feelings become actions. Our actions become reality. I encourage you to think differently, feel differently, act differently, and manifest differently for a life of true abundance.

Introduction
About This Guide

Picture this. You wake up in your bed, grateful to see another morning. You smile because you have health, purpose, and love. You no longer walk through the motions of each day in a zombie-like trance. You now take every opportunity to seize the day because you are the author of your amazing story. Quite a contrast to the state of being you may have been in after experiencing tragedy or heartbreak in your past. Our lives are a myriad of experiences and relationships, but it can be hard to experience great relationships with others if we struggle with loving and appreciating the most important person in our lives: ourselves.

In this guide, you will discover how to persist past pain and live powerfully after tragedy. By focusing on health, finances, and life itself you can overcome the deepest grief of your life. In creating the best relationship with yourself, the doors to your future endeavors will unlock. Improving the relationship with yourself will spill your cup of love into your finances, health, relationships, and overall satisfaction.

Through a series of six sessions, this workbook will provide a guided revelation of the aspects that make you the powerful individual that you are and the obstacles that you create to prevent you (and possibly others) from seeing that. The prompted self-analysis will target areas in where you can be more accountable and responsible for the direction of your life. As if that does not provide enough transformation, in addition to your reading of this book, you can also join an on-line or in-person workshop. In this seminar, I will guide you on your path to self-discovery where you will work on leaving the past behind you, creating powerful opportunities to improve your health and finances, and discovering your purpose to impact the lives of others.

Happiness is in the journey of finding yourself. The joy is in the doing.

Let's do it together!

Madi Still

A Promise for Me

I _____ promise
to complete the tasks in this book. I know that
transformation means taking responsibility and
accountability for myself. I know that to truly manifest
what is to come, I need to make changes with what is
here now and release myself from the pain of my past.

I will finish the work needed for this to happen.

_____

Signature

SESSION ONE

Connect

It was February 28, 2008 at 1:10 PM. I was standing in a darkened room, save for one bright light shining in the center. Chaos ebbed and flowed around me like a tornado, only it wasn't a car being tossed to the side or trees being uprooted; it was my heart being wrenched as I stood by helplessly watching doctors as they tried to save the life of my two-day-old son.

Months prior, things were about as normal as they could get. I was battling morning sickness daily, dreaming about the features my child would have, and patiently waiting for the day I could find out the sex of the baby. Would I decorate a nursery for a princess? Would she watch fairies dance on her wall and be doused in imaginary seeds from a dandelion being blown across her ceiling? Would I decorate a baby "boy cave"? Would there be ships? Sports helmets and gloves? Or would my son be a real-life action hero surrounded by Marvel comics, his Daddy's favorite?

One appointment in particular, however, changed the course of my normal pregnancy and sent us speeding into another dimension entirely. We were present to hear results from an amniocentesis that had given our obstetrician cause for concern. I sat across from one of the top specialists in the country, sitting tall as my father taught me, confident in God and the promise growing in my belly.

Candidly, she peered over her glasses and said, "Detach yourself from this pregnancy. Your baby will die in utero." I felt the lurch in my stomach, that violent wave of nausea that threatened to reveal pieces of my breakfast across her table. I wanted to ask her to repeat herself. Did she just use the words "detach and die?" I was sure I'd heard her correctly, but for whatever reason, I just could not process the conversation.

"You have what's called an insufficient placenta," she said. "Your placenta is incapable of providing proper nourishment and blood flow. Your baby won't be able to survive." All I heard was the word "insufficient." That word didn't just describe my placenta in that moment; it described me as a mother, a wife, a woman. I don't know that I'd ever felt more insufficient in my entire life than at that very moment.

For fifteen weeks we held out hope as small kicks began to grow in number within my belly. The specialist gave us no reason to hope. Each week was just as horrific as the last. There was no progress and no reason to believe he would survive. And yet, I continued to have faith. I was like most moms, becoming invested in my child. Daily I sang to him, read to him, felt him in my heart and soul. He was mine. I felt this huge responsibility to protect him and believe in him, despite the fact that no one else did.

On a cold February afternoon, amidst a room filled with nurses and doctors, Noah Abram Still was born. I wish I could say I felt relief when I saw him lying on a table beside me. I wish I could say I smiled when he kicked the nurse or when a doctor exclaimed "Oh my gosh, he can open his eyes." But I didn't. He was barely the size of my palm and a breathing tube was being inched into his esophagus. I didn't feel relief. I felt fear. Utterly, crippling fear.

Hours. That's all I have. 48 of them to be exact, but 48 hours I consider a gift, is what I spent with my Noah. Mothers in the NICU would cradle their children kangaroo style, and I would stare with envy. All I had was my index finger to gently caress the patches of hair growing on his head. I would stare at this baby, the smallest the hospital had ever seen, and pray I could hold on to him just a little longer, even a lifetime.

Two days of being his mother passed. Being his mother meant pumping milk every two hours in hopes that one day he would be able to drink. Being his mother meant calling the NICU every two hours to see if he was still alive. Being his mother meant sitting beside him caressing his hair with only one index finger. Quite frankly, it was exhausting.

February 28, 2008 arrived and with it, snow outside and coldness in my heart. While eating rubbery chicken fingers from the hospital cafeteria, we heard a faint knock on the door. A nurse stood with glazed, teary eyes and whispered, "They need you downstairs." Despite having had a c-section just two days prior, I had never run so fast in my entire life. When we entered the NICU, the entire room was dark, save for one bright light shining on my son's incubator. I thought, "this is it. He is dying. She was right." The specialist was right. He would die, just not at the time she anticipated. I knelt on all fours, gasping for air. A nurse came to my side and instructed me to stand. "Your son needs you." I wanted to scream, "I need him!"

How could I face this moment? How could I say goodbye?

We watched in horror as our son died, with his dad by his side and tearful doctors standing by in shock, for they too had started to hope. I recall the horrifying sounds of a woman screaming. The screams were like gut wrenching battle cries. Someone' soul was broken. As my husband held me on the floor I realized, that woman was me.

We spent hours on a forest-green, polyester couch holding our dead baby in our hands. I remember they had swaddled him in blankets and I was enraged. Didn't they know that for two days I had never had the opportunity to hold him? I just wanted to experience holding my son "kangaroo style" on my chest like all the other moms I enviously watched for two days did. I wanted to feel his skin, though cold now, against my chest. I wanted to memorize every feature of him, knowing I'd never see him again. What did his belly look like? Did he have any fat on his legs? Do premature babies have fat? I didn't know, but I had to explore him. I had to touch my nose to his. I had to rub my cheeks against his. I had to finger the patches of hair growing on his small head. Giving my son back to the nurses, saying goodbye for the last time, was and still is the hardest moment of my entire life.

How does someone move on? Perhaps you are a parent reading this and you're thinking "there's just no way I could survive that." The truth is, for months after Noah's death, I didn't see a way out either. Life was scary afterward. I became angry, bitter, resentful, lost, hopeless, and truly disempowered to live a life worth anything beyond what I had achieved. After all, I thought, what was the point? If God could take away my only child, what else would He take? What else would I not be allowed to have in life? What else did I even deserve? I began to partake in reckless behaviors. I would drink excessively and drive. I would do recreational drugs to numb the pain. I would take more Valium than prescribed. Anything to not feel. Long nights became longer days. Days turned into months. But I had to move on because life had to go on.

There's a secret I have for you. It's not told to people often enough in my opinion because we try to sugarcoat everything and make it seem "easier" for people to manage. So here it is, in plain text: sometimes life sucks. There. I said it. Sometimes, you won't get your way. Sometimes, you realize all you fought for won't come true. Sometimes, your baby dies. (How's that for candid?) So I have one question for you: how will you persist past pain?

If you die with whatever you were dreaming, you kill off any possibility for what's to come. Sure you can feel sad. What insane person wouldn't after experiencing the death of their child? But what's worse, the grief of now or the grief of forever? I could have chosen to live life upset, bitter, and blaming the world for the loss of Noah. His death could have ended my marriage because I blamed my husband for not grieving the way I did. Noah's death could have caused me anguish, I could have made the decision to never have another child again (thus never meeting my new son, DJ) But persisting past pain means choosing to get up. It doesn't matter how hard the fight; every champion can get up for another round. You may be asking one simple question by this point: "how?"

Connect with that pain and get angry with God. Yup. You heard me. Fight with God. Kneel in a room and scream those awful things you need to say. You can blame Him (temporarily) because I guarantee He can take it. He knows that is how you feel anyway. I had to tell Him how angry I was. How much I hated Him for taking away my baby. Some may disagree, but God knows your heart, so just be honest. Connect to the pain on a deep level. Some run from the pain. They run because it's too much to bear. What happens however is we begin to overcompensate for that in other areas of life. We may become bitter, angry, drug-addicted, etc. The connection is healthy. You begin to recognize the power of that person or event in your life and moving forward, you make life-changing decisions because of that connection. This book will give you five key steps to not only connecting to the pain, but overcoming it and discovering a purpose that impacts the world. Your painful event, no matter what it is, was designed for your life.

REFLECTION EXERCISE

What does it mean to you to "persist past pain"?

_____

_____

_____

_____

_____

_____

Session One

Connect

Welcome to our first session together.

Here we explore what it means to connect to our past, our pain,
and our feelings surrounding our journey to move forward.

We will trace the map of details aligned with our past,
and navigate through the maze to move forward.

We forgive.
We celebrate the gift of life.
We honor the foundation given to us.
We breath, we love, and we let go.

Task 1: The Roots

"Healing doesn't mean the damage never existed.
It means it no longer controls our lives."
~Anonymous

One reason many people cannot move forward with their purpose in life is they are still attached to the pain of their past. It is time to connect to that pain so we can utilize this experience to discover our purpose and use it to make a difference.

On the next page are some blank lines. Here is where healing can begin. For you to move forward, this step is crucial. I want you to connect to the pain or experience in your past that you still think about or feel holds you back in some way. Make sure you are alone in a quiet place. Use more paper if you need. Give yourself a time limit, set the timer, and do not allow your pen to stop. Even if you are writing "blah blah... I'm hungry... I don't want to do this..." keep writing until an idea comes to you and the timer stops. It is called stream of consciousness writing, where you just keep going, no matter what.

Warning: when we get too close to the pain, we have a tendency to withdraw. We may resist by watching TV, texting, web surfing, or putting the pen away. Take note of these occurrences, but DO NOT STOP WRITING.

Some ideas for writing prompts:
1. Write a letter to your former self from that time period. If you were a child, try an inner dialog with that child from the adult you are now.

2. Write a list to begin. Consider the who of that event, the what that happened, the why, the where, and the how it happened.

3. Write in third person. Detach yourself as the main character and insert your name. When you finish, erase your name and insert "I". Read this aloud and allow yourself to feel.

Task 1: The Roots

_____

_____

_____

_____

_____

_____

_____

_____

_____

_____

_____

_____

_____

Task 2: Reflect

Let's reflect on that experience. How was that for you? Write your response below.

_____

_____

_____

_____

_____

_____

_____

_____

_____

_____

_____

_____

_____

Task 3: Connect

How did this event connect you to the person or thing you experienced and how can the event connect you to fulfill a greater purpose in life?

_____

_____

_____

_____

_____

_____

_____

_____

_____

_____

_____

_____

_____

SESSION TWO

Strength

It was a typical afternoon and I was on a winding street heading toward my home. The trees blurred with a palette of fall colors. I could feel the dips and curves on the road, but as I continued driving, I could also feel those dips in my emotions. My palms were clammy. My breathing began to quicken and I suddenly felt an immense desire to pull over. I tried to calm the shallow breaths, but the wave of hysteria swept over me and I began to cry uncontrollably. After arriving home, I immediately fell to the floor in a fetal position and let the guttural cries from my chest explode while listening to my husband talk to a doctor about my current mental condition.

What I did not know then, was I was having my first panic attack, only five years after my son's death. But why? He'd been gone for five years, surely long enough for me to be "over it," right? I had a healthy, lively four-year-old at home. Our finances were beginning to turn around and we were slowly climbing out of debt. Why would this happen now?

In the three years since that episode, I have experienced a total of four of those same moments, though now I can recognize the signs much more quickly. At the time, doctors wanted me admitted to a facility (fearing I would endanger myself) and I toyed with the idea of just packing a bag and "getting away" I'm grateful for that first moment however, because it taught me a very important lesson in my journey of persisting past pain: that I am stronger than I thought and truly unbreakable.

Perhaps you survived some horrific accident or surgery and now must rely on physical therapy to build your muscles and regain some semblance of strength. Perhaps you sought out psychological therapy to strengthen your mind from a tragic breakup. Or if you're like me, you sought out church to strengthen your spirit. Had it not been for that event you experienced, You wouldn't even know how strong you truly are, nor how strong you can be for others.

Merely one year after Noah's death, my life dramatically changed again. My son DJ was born and with him, new dreams and new challenges as well. He brought a tornado of new experiences with him. From learning how to satisfy his nursing appetite to how to juggle laundry, work, exercise, motherhood (and dare I say it--- sex). I felt like I was a rookie at life and I complained daily about not being "taught" better for the change. I empathize with new mothers. No one tells us how hard it's going to be (and when they do we scoff, turn our noses up and convince ourselves they are wrong). No one tells us that we will dream of days when four hours sleep in a row is the norm. No one says that 24 hours per day is merely half the time that is actually needed. And more importantly, no one says that we can do it. We have been through worse, so nothing can stand in our way of whatever goal lies ahead.

I think being a mother is where I initially learned that in my strength, I had to incorporate self-care. I realized there is no such thing as "time." Sure there are hours, minutes, and seconds, but none of them really mattered when it came to self-care. As my sister used to say "I'll sleep when I'm dead." This became my life motto and I lived it everyday, 365 days a year, for five years. Well, I'm here to tell you that eventually, "time" will catch your ass and make you question your strength like never before.

Much like motherhood, entrepreneurs are taught (through our mentors both on and off YouTube) to chase the dream. We fight daily for the future and we often put more on our plates than many others could even fathom attempting. The problem with this is there are no books teaching the entrepreneur (or the mother) we need to *unplug* to regain our strength. No one says, "Take a day off". Instead it's the characteristic speech, "One day off can set your dreams back months!" No one ever says, "Hey, people die from being overworked, so make sure to take time for you." The guilt we often feel is heavy, but this modern *mompreneur* is here to tell you that a day off and time to yourself is just as vital as your days on. It's called recreation for a reason. Because we recreate ourselves in the rest we receive.

We tend to move so fast in life that it leads to stress, followed by lack of sleep, followed by overeating, and resulting in weight gain. There were days I was tired (even after sleeping eight hours), emotional (never understanding why on earth I was crying to a commercial on TV) and feeling like I had more on my to-do list than what actually was getting done. My strength was being tested.

So how do you combat these feelings of anxiety and stress? First, I got a planner. I found this one small step to be incredibly valuable. Scheduling my meals, my exercise, my time with my family, and prioritizing a to-do list actually made me feel more organized, thus leading to less anxiety and a stronger mindset. Secondly, I schedule Boss Time. Boss Time is one hour per day for *me* that no one can interrupt. I may read, listen to music, watch a few shows saved on my DVR, write in my gratitude journal, or take a walk outside and observe the nature around me. But this time is for *me* to restore my balance and energy. We have to protect our energy because whenever we change our inner frequency, it becomes a direct imbalance with the energy *outside*. We cannot give what we do not have. We do not have to feel guilty for saying "I matter." Your time matters. Your energy matters. Your mental health matters. *You matter.*

REFLECTION EXERCISE

What is one activity you can implement to find your strength?

_____

_____

_____

_____

_____

Take note of how you feel after this activity. Does it help you?

_____

_____

_____

_____

SESSION 2

Strength & Effectiveness

It's 5:25 AM. Sleepily I crack one eye open and reach for my phone. Slowly the other eye begins to open and I adjust to the light on my cell phone as I open my bible app. I turn to the scripture of the day and share on Facebook (a daily ritual I've practiced now for more than a year.) I spend ten minutes reading that day's devotional reading before willing myself out of bed and trekking downstairs for my energizing green tea. The rest of the hour consists of stating affirmations, posting a motivational, yet self-generated quote, and listening to personal development while preparing for my sixteen-hour day.

This has been every morning for the last three years. No day is successful without this morning ritual or the planning that takes place the night before. People often ask, "Madi, how do you do it?" They want to know how does someone survive the death of a child, go on to run a successful business, venture into more business options, keep a strong marriage, and overall survive life?

I give you, dear reader, six secrets to being strong and effective:

1. BALANCE

Repeat after me: there is no such thing as balance. If you are standing in the middle of two sides, you never truly give 100% to either side. We certainly wouldn't want 50% of a meal or 50% of a paycheck, so why would our families want half our time while we are "multi-tasking" by doing a job while "spending quality time" with our children? At any time of the day, you will have to CHOOSE which activity deserves 100% of your time and focus. Warning, that choice will often cause guilt due to the painful sacrifices you'll make. In the mornings, I am 100% me. Whether that is the gym, meditation, or just watching a TV show, I am completely consumed and obsessed with myself - and I don't feel guilty for that. You cannot develop strength for others if you feel weak physically, mentally, or spiritually.

After I have filled my cup, I am 100% entrepreneur. I am assisting clients, working on new blogs, assisting team members, leading conference calls, watching modules to become a better entrepreneur etc. I use these hours to build my income, but at night, I'm 100% mom, building my legacy. What use is income if your child hates you for the time you never spent at home? When I am mom, he is my only priority. I am not texting. I am not skyping. I am not facetiming. I am being a present parent, for that is my most important job.

Once I realized that I had to choose which activity got 100% of me, I found I was far less stressed trying to do the impossible (balancing it all.) Trying to balance only makes you feel incompetent, stressed, angry, anxious and more. Let the idea go that you can multi-task. Think of it this way: if you were lost on the highway and trying to find your way, how many addresses could your GPS navigate at one time? Unless you have the most advanced form of technology known to man, I would assume you'd answer one. It is the same with life. You can only follow one course of action at a time to get to your destination.

2. SELF-CARE

Would you ever expect a car to run without gas? Of course not (unless it's solar powered, and even then it needs the sun's energy to run.) I find that we expect more of our minds, bodies, and spirits than we do our own automobiles. I remember one day, after putting in twelve hours of *work* all day, I was extra moody. I was short with my husband and showed irritable impatience to my son. Every question they asked seemed more minor and insignificant than the last. In one particularly low moment, I threw my son's papers across our kitchen island, screamed that they were both annoying and ran upstairs crying. *That* is what happens when we don't give our bodies the fuel that helps us run and makes us feel good. Maybe like me, you need a thirty-minute quiet meditation period everyday to just find your peace. Maybe you need to exercise, watch TV, take a nap, act silly with a friend... Whatever that *thing* is, do it and do it *every day*.

3. SUPPORT SYSTEM

One thing I mentioned in my TEDx Talk: *Using Pain As a Bridge To Discovering Your Purpose*, is that if you are going to survive pain and use it to impact others, you need a strong system in place. The old adage, *it takes a village*, rings true; I have no idea how I would accomplish running my business, speaking to mothers about grief, raising a son, and supporting my husband if it were not for my village.

Every month, I attend a business training. Every Thursday night, I attend a networking event. How on earth could I do these things if it were not for the village who raises my son in the times I can't? I have to mention this also... do not choose a village keeper who judges you for the work you do. If my mother was always scolding me about the time I'm away from my son building my business (for him) then I would feel defeated. Find someone who not only supports your child, but supports your vision too.

In addition to the village, you need emotional support. Do you have a mentor? Someone who keeps your attitude and mind in check when things get tough? Do you have people who keep you humble and remind you where you came from, yet also support your dreams and pick you up when it gets too hard? Without these key people in place, you will struggle.

4. FILTERED VISION

When I think of the word *filter* I think of our air-conditioning system. Its purpose is to block harmful particles from entering our home, thereby allowing us to breath purified air. Shouldn't our vision be filtered of harmful substances also?

I am a firm believer in walking away from what does not elevate you. I've walked away from friends who no longer served me spiritually and mentally. Picture this, you are trying to expand your million dollar business, and you are sitting in a nightclub with people whose only concern in life is what the cost of a VIP bottle is. This happened to my husband and me one night in the city. We looked around us and thought "We don't belong here." In no way do I say this judgmentally. By all means everyone is entitled to the life that makes them happy; however, my mission in life is not to pop bottles. It's to pop souls. It's to pop my legacy. It's to drink from the stream of abundance. I can't drink overflow in a deserted wasteland.

We should have a system in place that blocks our vision from poison like cancerous people, negative TV shows that do not add to your growth, outings that put you in atmospheres with people who operate on a lower frequency than you. When your vision is filtered, you have a one-track mind that is purpose-filled. Anything that tries to penetrate that vision is toxic and should be blocked from entering. One way to filter your vision is to write a vision statement/mission statement for your life. That vision statement should guide everything you do. If you are out with others, ask yourself, does this support my vision statement? If the answer is no, you know you need to re-evaluate your filtering system.

5. A STRONG WHY

If your why does not make you emotional, passionate, prompt you into action, excite you, or force you to work harder, it is not your true why. Don't feel guilty if your child(ren) is not your why. For some, we love our children, but what wakes us up or gives us our strength after our painful event is not directly correlated with our children. For instance, my why is to leave my thumbprint on this world. I get excited beyond belief when people say "I watch your video blogs every week and they get me through my days." When I hear things like that, a fire ignites in my soul. It makes me want to continue working to ensure that I touch millions who eventually feel the same way. Does your why do that? Does it ignite a burning passion inside you that somehow begins the healing process of your past?

6. DIVINE UNDERSTANDING OF SELF

Who you are needs to be very clear to you and others. When you have a divine sense of self, you understand who you were created to be. For instance, when I was a child, I talked a lot. I would follow my mother from room to room dragging my chair behind. As an adolescent, I would receive the same comment on every report card, "Her talking is disruptive in class." As a high school senior, I was voted most talkative. It's no accident I became a teacher at the age of 23, a profession where selling yourself and casting vision to youth requires *talking*. I didn't know then, but my disrupt in the classroom was preparing me for the disrupt of people's souls with my speaking. You have to understand you have a divine responsibility to carry out the purpose you've been given and ignoring that God-given purpose will bring not just a void in life, but struggle as well.

REFLECTION EXERCISE

Which of the six secrets above gives you the most struggle in your business/personal life?

_____

_____

Session Two

Strength

Welcome to Session Two of our journey together.
Here we explore basic fundamentals in life
related to our health and self-care...
two essential areas to strengthen our spirit.

We practice awareness of our health.
We create new habits for success.
We find value in self-care.
We work to connect the pieces missing.

Let the transformation begin.

MY DAILY FOOD LOG

Welcome to Session Two of your journey to self discovery. The truth is, people do not recognize the connection between their health and moving forward in life. If you are struggling with fatigue, headaches, etc, how can you perform at your best? How can you feel happy if everyday you feel sick? This session's focus is on our health. Below is a food log. Complete the log according to what your typical "food day" is like.

MEAL 1 — _ _: _ _ **AM**

MEAL 2 — _ _: _ _ **AM**

MEAL 3 — _ _: _ _ **PM**

MEAL 4 — _ _: _ _ **PM**

MEAL 5 — _ _: _ _ **PM**

MEAL BUILDER

Not sure how to eat? No problem. Add one item from each column to create a full meal. Use the food chart on the next page and this plan. Create a new week with these healthy, well-balanced meals. How does it compare to your previous habits? Remember this:

"A healthy outside starts from the inside."
- Robert Urich

PROTEINS
- egg whites
- lean beef
- chicken
- nuts
- ground turkey
- peanut butter
- beans
- dairy
- lamb
- pork
- lentils
- Ezekiel bread
- ground chicken
- turkey
- hemp seed
- quinoa
- cottage cheese
- protein powders
- chia seeds
- soybeans
- fish
- tofu

CARBS
- dark leafy greens
- fruits
- vegetables
- whole barley
- multigrain bread
- popcorn
- granola
- brown rice
- wild rice
- jasmine rice
- dairy
- quinoa
- oats
- couscous
- beans
- whole grain cereals
- sweet potatoes
- whole grain pasta
- rice cakes
- potatoes

FATS
- olive oil
- hummus
- peanut butter
- avocado
- nut butter
- coconut oil
- cheese
- seeds
- nuts
- eggs

VEGGIES
- spinach
- cucumbers
- green beans
- eggplant
- lettuce
- broccoli
- cauliflower
- asparagus
- squash
- kale
- peas
- artichoke
- cabbage
- tomatoes
- arugula
- peppers
- soybeans
- celery
- carrots

MY IDEAL FOOD LOG

Utilizing the "Build a Meal" plan, create an ideal food log. Envision yourself healthier, happier, and making good choices that help you function in your day to day living.

"Take care of your body. It's the only place you have to live."
- Jim Rohn

MEAL 1 _ _: _ _ **AM**

MEAL 2 _ _: _ _ **AM**

MEAL 3 _ _: _ _ **PM**

MEAL 4 _ _: _ _ **PM**

MEAL 5 _ _: _ _ **PM**

SELF-CARE CHECKLIST

Let's evaluate your methods of self-care.

"Love yourself first, and everything else falls in line.
You really have to love yourself to get anything done in this world."
- Lucille Ball

RATING SYSTEM
SA: Strongly Agree   A: Agree   U: Unsure   D: Disagree   SD: Strongly Disagree

I get 6 - 8 hours sleep every night	SA	A	U	D	SD
I have one hour per day to myself doing something I enjoy	SA	A	U	D	SD
I eat well and exercise regularly	SA	A	U	D	SD
I read/listen to books to develop my mind and spirit	SA	A	U	D	SD
I spend time with loved ones daily	SA	A	U	D	SD
I have a spiritual practice that brings me peace	SA	A	U	D	SD
I have a daily practice to express gratitude	SA	A	U	D	SD
I laugh every day	SA	A	U	D	SD
I have a strong circle of friends	SA	A	U	D	SD
I handle anger and stress in a healthy way	SA	A	U	D	SD

Based on your answers, what have you discovered about your methods of self care?

_____

_____

_____

_____

Are there areas in your self-care methods that could be holding you back from living a successful, happy life? If so, which areas?

_____

_____

_____

_____

List three action steps you will take to improve in those areas:

1. _____

_____

2. _____

_____

3. _____

_____

SELF-CARE CHECKLIST

*"I believe the greatest gift you can give your family
and the world is a healthy you."*
- Joyce Meyer

RATING SYSTEM
SA: Strongly Agree   A: Agree   U: Unsure   D: Disagree   SD: Strongly Disagree

I understand the connection between my diet and my performance	SA	A	U	D	SD
I track my daily diet and make adjustments where needed	SA	A	U	D	SD
Exercise is important to me	SA	A	U	D	SD
I believe my mental health is critical to my well being	SA	A	U	D	SD
I drink more than 8 glasses of water daily	SA	A	U	D	SD
I have health changes I need to make	SA	A	U	D	SD
I am confident with my body	SA	A	U	D	SD
I believe in accountability for my health	SA	A	U	D	SD
I sometimes experience physical issues related to my health	SA	A	U	D	SD

HEALTH AFFIRMATIONS

Affirmations are not just statements we make to make ourselves pretend to feel better; affirmations are REAL. When we envision ourselves where we want to be or we express an affirmation with firm belief, we change the frequency in our brain to operate at a higher level and we begin to attract what it is we want. I'm not just a believer of this; I've experienced it. Have you ever thought, "Oh, it would be awesome to have a parking spot open as soon as I get there," and it happens? Or how about the opposite? Have you ever said, "I never get parking" and no spot is available? It's true, our thoughts become real and what we feel when we think and say those things is when true transformation begins. Below, list 5 - 10 affirmations you wish to make about your health. For example: "I love every piece of myself and care for my temple daily."

1. _____

2. _____

3. _____

4. _____

5. _____

6. _____

7. _____

8. _____

9. _____

10. _____

SESSION THREE

Desire

So you have connected to the pain. You've seen strength in yourself you didn't even know you had. Now what? After you've gotten rid of the rage and identified the strength, understand that pain leads to a life-changing decision: the desire to seek happiness. Three years after the birth of my second son, DJ, I began to feel a vapid emptiness. It wasn't from grief; it was from a nagging feeling that I was supposed to be doing more. Have you ever wondered, "God, is this it?" Perhaps you are a mom and your kids are needing you less and less, so you are wondering, what is out there for me? Your desire was fulfilling the needs of your children/spouse and now you have no clue what your needs are. Perhaps you are in a career that no longer brings you joy. You go to work everyday feeling as if the shoe no longer fits. You desires are changing and with that, depression is seeping in.

86, 400. That's the number of seconds we have everyday. The problem with time is we often take it for granted (cliché, I know.) We think we have so much time that we waste the seconds given to us in a job we no longer even like. We borrow time from the next day when in reality, time is a one-time deposit into your daily balance that cannot be transferred to another day. We make statements like, "I'll do that tomorrow" or "I'll let you know if I can make it later this week" and worse, "I'll find a new job eventually." What if tomorrow, or a few hours, or eventually never comes? Morbid, I know, but every day you decide to *borrow time* you set yourself up for disappointment. You don't actually know your *end-dash* date so how can you be arrogant enough to think you can control your time?

The true reward of seeking happiness is utilizing your time in those activities that bring your purpose and joy. You are rewarded with the daily work and effort you put forth in chasing your desires. For me, I became obsessed with the gym. There was something comforting about picking up heavy weights and slamming them back to the ground. I also became just as obsessed with the atmosphere. People from different backgrounds all working toward one common goal: becoming a healthier person. Sometimes however, we waste precious moments discovering our purpose and we stop spending our time where that time matters: our family and our peace. I'm here to tell you that you *can* use time wisely to discover your happiness and purpose by utilizing two key things: motivation and appreciation.

First, you have to get motivated. A lot of my clients say things like, "I need help finding my motivation." Here's the problem: I can't find what you can't produce. What do you need to reach out to, grab, and hold on tight? What will get you to climb out of bed and stop wasting the precious seconds in your morning? Don't give an answer that others would say. What makes you tick? For me, it's knowing I don't have a choice. There is no Plan B for my life. The opportunity I'm working on now is my *only* chance at making it. If I don't seize these seconds, I lose it all. That creates in me a sense of urgency but also a sense of exhilarating joy. I don't have time to be lazy, apathetic, or doubtful. I appreciate every second because every second is a second to fulfilling my life desire to be happier than I have ever been. I use to-do lists so that my time is shaped in a constructive manner and I make sure that 65% or more of time is dedicated to one of the following: serving others, bettering myself, family, and chasing my dreams.

Another area I spend my time is in the value of appreciating more. Have you ever spent time taking a walk outside alone to admire trees, flowers, buildings, etc? How often do you pass the same park everyday and not once stop to just be alone in your thoughts. We get so caught up in social media and the smokescreen of what we believe is reality that we fail to appreciate what we have right in front of us. Prime example, someone posts a picture of their new home. Rather than spending time appreciating your home and the laughter or love it contains, you spend time grinding yourself to a pulp to get something better. Why do we do these things? Why do we spend our precious moments surfing Instagram for distorted views of a "perfect life"? Four years ago, I was in the worst financial strain of my entire life. My husband was out of work and we were barely surviving on my salary. Though it was stressful, scary, and at times hopeless, we found ways to appreciate the small things. We did not have money to eat at restaurants, so we found ways to cook as a family the items we could afford. We did not have the means to travel, so we found short day trips to take. It was to the point my son never lacked a thing. We put more value in memories than things. I believe that us experiencing this hardship was for our best. One year after our lowest period, we doubled our salary in our business, but money no longer controlled us. Being broke taught us to appreciate money, but not obsess over it. It taught us the value of time, not just the things we could fill a home with.

I must emphasize however that our financial demise was self-induced. We weren't just young and in love; we were young and plain ol' dumb. We wanted the very best as a young, married couple hopelessly in love. We wanted to immediately furnish our entire home with nothing but the best. We wanted to travel, own expensive cars and motorcycles and live a million dollar life on a minimum wage lifestyle. All of this would have been okay I suppose, had my husband not lost his job. But that's it; you never prepare for the worst. You don't expect life to fall apart and you certainly don't expect it to happen after the birth of your child.

Learning how to survive without money was the greatest lesson in our path to desiring more for our lives. I cringe thinking about what would have happened, had we started our business with the amount of income we made that first year, had we not learned the hard lesson of living with less. This is what many don't talk about. We don't talk about the fact that if you desire to live a powerful life, you need to not only get your health in check, not only get your time in check, but you need to get your money in check. You can't finance a dream with empty accounts and empty vision. So as we explore this session, I encourage you to allow the discomfort and commit to change. Having power in these areas will free you in more ways than you can imagine.

REFLECTION EXERCISE

Imagine your day is split into a pie chart. This pie chart encompasses all that makes you happy. I want you to create a pie chart with your sections of happiness. Once you have done that, I would like you to use the daily planner to record what a day in your life looks like. Be honest and open in this exercise. Once you have planned a typical day, I want you to highlight on that planner anything that is not listed in your pie chart. These are the items that are either not bringing you joy or they do not serve in your purpose. These are things you could consider removing from your day to day or at least adjusting.

Here is an example of my own pie chart.

Complete this blank chart with what is important to you and brings you purpose and joy.

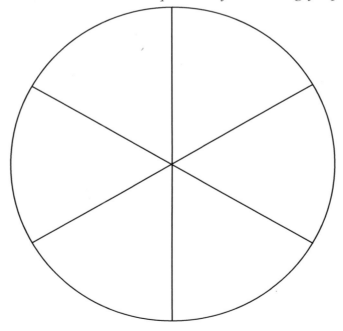

REFLECTION EXERCISE

Now go back to your day and highlight anything that is not listed in your pie chart. These are the items that are either not bringing you joy or they do not serve in your purpose. These are things you might want to remove from your day to day or at least consider adjusting. Journal below about your findings and what you seek to change for the better.

_____

_____

_____

_____

_____

_____

_____

_____

_____

_____

_____

_____

_____

_____

Session Three

Desire

Welcome to session three of our journey together.

Here we explore how our time and money
stops us from moving forward.
We identify the areas of need.
We create exciting solutions.
We recognize our relationship to money.
We replant a new foundation and we move forward.

DAILY SCHEDULE

"Time is a created thing. To say, 'I don't have time'
is to say, 'I don't want to.'"
- Lao Tzu

Below is a daily schedule. Record what a day in your life looks like. Be honest and open in this exercise.

6 AM

_____

7 AM

_____

8 AM

_____

9 AM

_____

10 AM

_____

11 AM

_____

12 PM

_____

1 PM

_____

2 PM

_____

3 PM

_____

4 PM

_____

5 PM

_____

6 PM

_____

7 PM

_____

8 PM

_____

9 PM

_____

FINANCIAL ASSESSMENT

Let's examine your finances to see what could be holding you back from success and happiness.

"Beware of little expenses. A small leak will sink a great ship."
- Benjamin Franklin

RATING SYSTEM
SA: Strongly Agree   A: Agree   U: Unsure   D: Disagree   SD: Strongly Disagree

I am financially stable	SA	A	U	D	SD
I have enough savings for six months income	SA	A	U	D	SD
I avoid credit cards for expenses	SA	A	U	D	SD
I own at least one credit card	SA	A	U	D	SD
I use a monthly budgeting system	SA	A	U	D	SD
I have a debt repayment plan	SA	A	U	D	SD
I have low interest rates for my car, house, etc.	SA	A	U	D	SD
I have a retirement savings plan	SA	A	U	D	SD
I have life insurance	SA	A	U	D	SD
I avoid impulse buying	SA	A	U	D	SD
I have a 5 year, 10 year, and 15 year plan for my money	SA	A	U	D	SD

Based on your answers, what has this survey revealed to you about your relationship to money?

_____

_____

_____

_____

_____

_____

_____

Do you see anything from your survey you know could be problematic and would like to change? List those areas here.

_____

_____

_____

_____

_____

_____

_____

SMART SPENDING

"You must gain control over your money, or the lack of it will forever control you."
- Dave Ramsey

Assess the last 30 days of your spending. Complete the chart below to help you become more fiscally aware and responsible.

INCOME ITEM	GOAL	ACTUAL
SALARY/HOURLY WAGES		
SUPPLEMENTAL INCOME 1		
SUPPLEMENTAL INCOME 2		
OTHER INCOME		

SPENDING ITEM	GOAL	ACTUAL
HOUSING/LIVING		
CAR/TRAVEL		
CAR INSURANCE		
CREDIT CARDS		

SMART SPENDING

Continued...

SPENDING ITEM	GOAL	ACTUAL
CHILDCARE		
LIFE INSURANCE		
CELL PHONE(S)		
GAS		

SPENDING ITEM	GOAL	ACTUAL
GROCERIES		
HOUSEHOLD ITEMS		
CLOTHING		
DINING OUT		

INCOME AFFIRMATIONS

As mentioned with the health survey, affirmations are real thoughts that become real "things". There is no difference in stating a strong belief with your health as there is with stating a strong belief for your finances. Have you ever thought about an amount you desperately need and suddenly receive a check for that amount? Have you ever said, "Money flows in my life" and the next day find money in your pocket you forgot about? I have and I believe this is from what I attract.

Create three affirmations related to your income. Here is a sample:

I attract an abundance of money daily and easily.

1. _____

2. _____

3. _____

Create three affirmations that empower your spending. Here is a sample:

I am fiscally responsible and secure in my finances.

1. _____

2. _____

3. _____

MY PLAN

Below write a plan for how you will stick to your monthly spending goals. For example, when I shop, I go to discount stores and dollar stores first. I get the items I need there to start, and then I go to the grocery store. I also come prepared with a shopping list so I don't get distracted. Lastly, I don't food shop when I'm hungry! Another tip is to keep only cash in an envelope for your flexible spending. Once that cash is gone, so is your flexible spending. What other tips can you provide for yourself below?

MY POWERFUL PLAN:

_____

_____

_____

_____

_____

_____

_____

_____

_____

_____

_____

MY PLAN

Now that you examined your spending, you can now begin saving. First, let's focus on why saving is important. Do you recall a time when you needed income but had no savings? Write about this experience below.

_____

_____

_____

_____

_____

_____

_____

_____

_____

_____

_____

_____

_____

_____

MY PLAN

What did it feel like for you?

_____

_____

_____

_____

_____

_____

_____

How did you overcome this?

_____

_____

_____

_____

_____

_____

SMART SAVINGS

Below is a table of "savings tips." Take a look at your spending budget and see where you can save.

ITEM	TYPICAL COST	THIS WEEK
CREDIT CARDS APR		
GIFTS		
DINING OUT		
SUBSCRIPTIONS		

ITEM	TYPICAL COST	THIS WEEK
MEMBERSHIPS		
CABLE TV		
CLOTHING		
OTHER		

SMART SAVINGS

Now list your savings goals and begin working a plan to make it happen.

ITEM	3-6 MOS PLAN	6-12 MOS PLAN
VACATION		
EMERGENCY FUND		
SPECIAL EVENTS		
BUSINESS START UP		

ITEM	3-6 MOS PLAN	6-12 MOS PLAN
NEW HOME/REPAYMENT		
EARLY RETIREMENT		
NEW CAR		
OTHER		

ENVISIONING EXERCISE

Now I want you to envision life with all your goals met. What would it look like for you to have all the money you want in savings? I want you to write a letter to someone (anyone you choose) as if all your goals have been met. Speak in past language, as if it has already happened. i.e. "I am so grateful that I saved over $5,000 to take my family on vacation!" Then I want you to read this letter everyday for 30 days. Begin to take notice of new happenings that begin to manifest in your life.

_____

_____

_____

_____

_____

_____

_____

_____

_____

_____

_____

ENVISIONING EXERCISE

_____

_____

_____

_____

_____

_____

_____

_____

_____

_____

_____

_____

_____

_____

_____

_____

_____

_____

_____

SESSION FOUR

Passion

Mel Robbins, wife to public figure and motivational speaker Tony Robbins, once gave a TED talk entitled "How To Stop Screwing Yourself Over." In this dynamic presentation, she mentions the biggest problem men and women face today: The *F* word. Now before you get your mind in the gutter, she's not referring to *that F* word. This *F* word is one of the most powerfully used words in human vocabulary: *Fine*.

I remember how often I used that word months after Noahs' death. At work they'd ask, "How are you?" "Fine" I'd numbly respond. Truth? I wasn't fine. I had milk in my breasts and no baby to nurse. I had diapers in a closet with no baby to change. I had an empty nursery only filled with his ashes. At night, I would dream of him. He would gently sleep in the cradle of my arm and I would smile at the face that was a perfect balance of his mother and father. Then my husband would move or cough and I would wake to an empty room and emptier arms. I would then be overcome by grief and holler in woeful tears only to be rocked back to sleep and told, "It's okay."

How many times has someone asked you, "How are you" to which you respond, "Fine." Consider the amount of times you've gotten into an argument and ended your battle with *fine*, and walked away. *Fine* is the final white flag. The surrendered soul. The *I've given up on this* of all conversations. I've got a little secret for you however; *fine* is also the word that crushes dreams, aspirations, and purpose.

That purpose begins to lead to your life-long passion and the reason you experienced the pain from your past to begin with. For me, years after Noah's death, I wanted to do something that mattered. I wanted people to find their hope, their strength, their power. Would I have been able to do that had Noah been here, alive but disabled? Perhaps. But in his death, ideas and conversations and new plans were born. My life work is all I think of now. It wakes me up in the middle of the night. It calls to me in my dreams. It's in that moment where you can recognize the pain you felt, the memory you were connected to, it's led you to your purpose. You discover that in that passion, your true purpose in life is whatever lies *under* that pain. And you seek it for the rest of your life, because helping others find their peace is now easier than living in your own chaos.

Fine is directly related to the idea of complacency. When you're fine, you're saying you're satisfied with your life right where it is. You're fine with the extra pounds you've put on (or insert whatever reason for you feeling *fine* here.) You're *fine* working at the job that makes you miserable. You're *fine* being in a marriage in which you no longer find satisfaction. As long as things are *fine* you will never live a truly fulfilling life. There's power in *not* being *fine*. There is power in your vulnerability. When you can finally say, "Hey, things are *not* okay. I am *not fine*. I am *not* happy this way," you give power to your words, your beliefs, and eventually your actions.

Recognizing I was not *fine* was how I found my grief support group and began to work on truly healing. That room, with all those mothers who lost their children too, became a safe space for me. They would share their stories about their own pain and I would find solace in that. I know, what cruel person finds peace in someone's pain? But we all did, because we weren't alone. We had the story of someone else to hold onto. Someone else wondered why. Someone else hated other pregnant women too (a thought I had frequently during that time).

The first step to breaking the bond of complacency and discovering your passion is recognizing where in life you are not fine. Where have you had to convince yourself? Where have you had to pretend happiness for the sake of peace elsewhere? Possibly the more damaging *F* word is *fake*. We don't want to admit we are *fake*. In fact, we may brag with others about *keepin' it real* when in actuality we lie everyday. We lie about our happiness so that we protect the happiness of others. At some point in your younger life, you convinced yourself that upsetting others was bad, so you avoided doing so by lying behind being *fine*. Or perhaps you convince yourself that if you reveal to someone your true feelings, they won't like you anymore.

In reality however, anyone whoever does not accept your true feelings is someone not worthy of your love to begin with. We restructure our very own beliefs and personal morals for the sake of accommodating someone else. By doing so, by faking it and hiding behind *fine*, we become angry, distant, bitter, and overall out of integrity. When out of integrity with the person you truly are inside, by projecting this *fake* image, you silence yourself and become irrelevant. Who can possibly take you seriously if every time a disagreement arises, you're just *fine*? People are not happy with *yes* men. People want true, authentic, real. The best friendships and relationships are the ones with authentic exchanges, no matter how much the verbiage may hurt in an uncomfortable conversation.

Consider your closest friendships. What adds depth and meaning to the friendship is the realness that is associated with it. You appreciate these friendships because in your lowest points, you grow through your pain because of the truths revealed in those authentic conversations. The friend you go to doesn't just say *fine*. They help you mature, they help you grow, they help you redefine your psyche in some instances. It is time to drop the facade of fine and pick up the authentic self hiding inside. It is time to live more powerfully and admit, you are not fine and you will not settle for fine any longer.

REFLECTION EXERCISE

Make a list of your passions in life. Identify the things you deem "fine" and connect how that list could be impacting your passion. For example, you may say your health is fine, but tend to ignore the number of days you struggle with exhaustion, depression, etc.

_____

_____

_____

_____

_____

_____

_____

_____

_____

Session Four

Passion

Welcome to session four.
In this session we will explore our passion
and how that connects to the journey ahead.

We will evaluate our inner selves.
We will make the connection between our true selves,
and how we communicate with those we love.
We will find our voice.
We will celebrate our means to success.

PREP PROFILE

One of the areas we deem as "fine" are the relationships we have with others. We sometimes don't realize that we positively impact those relationships just by having a deeper understanding of our authentic selves. Below is a sort-of personality assessment. This is the beginning of self-awareness. Check all that apply to yourself in each category.

CATEGORY ONE

- [ ] I love to be in the spotlight
- [ ] I am motivated by fun
- [ ] I love to dance
- [ ] I can be disorganized at times
- [ ] I prefer working in groups
- [ ] I am a free spirit
- [ ] I often have a positive outlook

CATEGORY TWO

- [ ] I am competitive
- [ ] I like a challenge
- [ ] I thrive off pressure to succeed
- [ ] I dislike complacent people
- [ ] As a child I was a sore loser
- [ ] I develop and chase goals daily
- [ ] I am mistaken as insensitive

CATEGORY THREE

- [ ] I am mistaken as cold
- [ ] I have trouble sleeping
- [ ] I am an organized person
- [ ] I love systems like Excel
- [ ] I use a planner/to-do lists daily
- [ ] I am considered analytical
- [ ] I consider problems from all angles

CATEGORY FOUR

- [ ] I am an introvert
- [ ] I am motivated by purpose
- [ ] I like being alone
- [ ] I feel awkward in groups
- [ ] I am patient and thoughtful
- [ ] I stay calm under pressure
- [ ] I love helping people

PREP PROFILE

CATEGORY TWO

(P)OWER LEADERS

These leaders are motivated by challenges and goals. They must succeed because they are natural leaders and competitors. They have incredible drive and they resist people who are not self-motivated. They love recognition and they will not play "the game" unless they can win.

CATEGORY FOUR

(R)ELATABLE LEADERS

These leaders strive to be a part of something bigger than themselves. They are most likely introverted, dependable and calm. They prefer small gatherings and are motivated by helping others. They dislike confrontation and they seek true change for the people.

CATEGORY THREE

(E)XPLORATIVE LEADERS

These leaders are motivated by facts and figures. They love to analyze, plan ahead, organize and have systematic ways of doing things. They are typically on time and need to know all the details prior to starting a project. They explore every detail and find solutions to problems.

CATEGORY ONE

(P)OPULAR LEADERS

These leaders are motivated by fun. They love to be the center of attention and they crave positive environments and circumstances. They strongly dislike rules and schedules. They can be a bit disorganized, but their energy is contagious.

PREP PROFILE REFLECTION

MY PRIMARY PREP PROFILE:

MY SECONDARY PREP PROFILE:

Now that you have identified yourself as one of the leaders in the PREP profile, I'd like you to write below how your profile...

1. *Limits your success*
2. *Helps your success*
3. *Impacts your relationship with others (i.e. spouse, coworkers, employees, family and friends)*

_____

_____

_____

_____

_____

_____

_____

_____

_____

_____

_____

SESSION FIVE

Purpose

Flowers. Amazing creations aren't they? A gardener plants seeds, waters those seeds, ensures proper sunlight, and then those seeds grow into fragile stalks with petals sprouting from the top. They have beautiful, unique scents and no two flowers are ever really the same. What is it about these flowers that make them so unique besides their color, scent, and appearance? It's *where* and *how* they grow.

For flowers to grow, they must have proper soil. Can a flower grow in concrete? It needs soft, nurturing soil to fulfill its purpose. So let me ask you: why are you still trying to grow in concrete? You have been growing in the same garden for so long, you don't even know you're allowed to move. As famous philosopher Jim Rohn would say, "You're not a tree." You don't have to stay where there's no sunlight, no water for growth, and no proper soil. You cannot live in your purpose without the fertile ground. You don't have to stay where people don't nourish you with love, support, and the ability to grow in *your* best setting.

We live in a world where mediocrity is acceptable. We give trophies to *both* teams because they both put up a good effort. We say, "Oh, it's okay. You gave it your best try." I'm not insinuating that we shouldn't celebrate small victories; however, should we celebrate them so much that one doesn't ever strive for more? It seems in this day and age, the greater you are, the more hate you receive. So we tend to stay in our non fertile soil because it's safe and we fear *out-blooming* other flowers.

It's time to disrupt your soil, reader, and discover your true purpose. It's time to unearth your old soil. It's time to move. Now when you do so, here's one key thing to remember: there will still be dirt. In order to grow, you still need to push through the dirt that gets piled on top of you. You will be buried in darkness. You will be thirsty for nourishment. This could be your finances, poor relationship, or a job you don't necessarily enjoy. But the exciting news is that when you push through, with proper nourishment in the right circumstances, you will bloom more beautifully. You have to push through dirt to grow.

In 2013, I was in non-fertile soil. I was malnourished in my job. I was searching for new sunlight to bring me to life. I took a chance by uprooting myself and planting *myself* in a new garden. When I became a mompreneur however, more dirt was thrown on top of me than I could have ever imagined. People talked about me, people hated me, some of my friends left me, and even some family members treated me differently. The beauty is, the more I push through that dirt, the more I felt myself bloom. I'm starting to understand the soil I come from. I have sunlight, personal development. I have the right water to nourish me, people in the right places. I have the right soil, my purpose.

If you want new, you have to move. No flower can grow to its fullest potential in concrete, not even weeds.

REFLECTION EXERCISE

You have journaled about your pain and come to the end of your journey in self-discovery. How can the pain you experienced in your past define your purpose today? For instance my son's death led to my life work of restoring and empowering others. What will be your life work?

_____

_____

_____

_____

_____

_____

_____

Session Five

Purpose

Welcome to session five,
where we now connect to the story and reveal it to others.

We will learn the art of story-telling.
We will stand secure in our truth.
We will identify our voice.
We will inspire others to find their own.

PREP'N & STORYTELLING

MAKING YOUR STORY MATTER

You have now traveled on the bridge from your pain to your purpose. You've discovered yourself in a new way. It's time to share your story. You may be asking "why" and getting a small lump in the base of your throat. Consider this: there is power in your vulnerability. There is a reason you are still here, on this Earth, reading this guide at this moment. Your story can impact the lives of others, but not if you keep quiet.

Note: If you are a business owner, the art of storytelling is even more important for you. Your openness and relatability will be the very thing to attract your audience.

THE PREP'N WAY TO TELL A STORY

Below is a PREP'n formula you can use when storytelling. Consider the following:

(P)ERSON: Who is the person to whom you are telling your story? This is your target audience. In developing my story about my son's death, my person is a grieving mother.

(R)ELATIONSHIP: This is the point where you establish a relationship with your person. How do you empathize with your person? Relate to your person here.

(E)XPERT: Why are you the expert in helping your person? This is where you show your expertise in your field/craft.

(P)RESENT: Present to your person what makes you the one to help.

(N)OTICE: This is your call to action, where you tell your person to take notice of what they want and take decisive action.

PREP'N & STORYTELLING

Below I share my own PREP story as an example and guide to helping you develop yours. Take notice of each step in the storytelling process:

Perhaps you are reading this and you lost someone in your life or experienced a tragic event, and that event brought you significant pain and grief. Perhaps you are someone who is searching for your purpose in this world, or you know someone hurting right now, struggling to find purpose in the pain. I invite you to watch my recently released TEDx Talk, *Using Pain as a Bridge to Discovering Your Purpose.*

Like you, I too have experienced trauma in my life. In my TEDx Talk, I share the tragic experience of watching my son die, and how that pain was actually a bridge to my purpose today.

I urge you to watch this ten-minute video and to share it to your social media pages and friends circle to inspire others to find *their* purpose for their pain.

Ten years later, my son's message still lives on. I pray it serves its purpose in your heart and for those you care for.

NOW IT IS YOUR TURN

It's time to craft your story and truly discover your greater "self." There are a few ways you can share...

1. Create a blog article
2. Create a video sharing your story on social media
3. Create a business plan or introduce a "big idea". What problem can your idea solve in the world that relates to your passion and purpose?

On the next page, craft your story/big idea. This could be the beginning of your destiny fulfilled. Remember to use your PREP exercise to speak directly to your target audience.

STORYTELLING EXERCISE

"To hell with facts! We need stories!"
- Ken Kesey

(P)ERSON - *Who is the person to whom you are telling your story?*

(R)ELATIONSHIP - *How do you empathize? Relate to your person here.*

(E)XPERT - *Why are you the expert in helping your person?*

(P)RESENT - *Present to your person what makes you the one to help.*

(N)OTICE - *Now tell your person to notice what they want and take action.*

MY STORY

Now it's your turn to create your own PREP story...

_____

_____

_____

_____

_____

_____

_____

_____

_____

_____

_____

_____

_____

_____

_____

_____

MY STORY

How will you use your PREP story to serve and benefit others?

_____

_____

_____

_____

_____

_____

_____

_____

_____

_____

_____

_____

_____

_____

SESSION SIX

His Gift. My Purpose.

We often begin each quest for change invested, passionate, and excited. Perhaps we attend a conference that we leave *fired up*. Maybe we listen to or watch a motivational video and think, "That's it. I'm making that change today!" You may even have come to this end and said, "I know what to do now." The problem is, feelings change. They wear off like in any relationship. The excitement can't possibly last forever because reality hits and we are faced with the complications that come with our commitments.

We make decisions initially on our feelings, but how do we remain committed when we just don't feel like it? How do you get up, day in and day out for that 5 AM workout when it's cold, raining, and the bed is beckoning you to stay just one more hour? How do we go out and produce just one more sale when we are tired of the rejection? How do we pull ourselves away from the distractions and push ourselves to work when there is no one there to tell us to or a video to motivate us into action?

The answer is pretty simple: we have to because it's our purpose. I know full well that not everyone is built of steel. There are people who will truly believe that they want something, but because of their own past or lack of integrity, they will crumble when the winds shake. I recently heard that success is a choice. We have to choose it daily. To some, failing does not hurt as much as it does to others. To me, failure kills me. Knowing I did not persevere at something and give it my all crushes my spirit. It keeps me awake. It drives me to give 10% more the next day. Failure is not the option for me. To me, there is no plan B. Why do some even bother to give a plan B? It is because they are afraid to fail at plan A. If you are anything like me however, you don't even consider failing as something possible. You know that the romance of your decision will fade, like any new love, but the resolve to win and the determination to succeed in living out your purpose will far outweigh the butterflies in your stomach initially. Those hard, pressing times will motivate you even more. You'll say to yourself more often than not, "I won't be beaten."

There is something deep down in us all, and that something is the desire to be more, do more, live more. We were not created to be miserable, hopeless creatures. Think of all the amazing triumphs we have seen as a human race because of the tenacity of the human spirit: we have electricity, the English language, the ability to fly by air, the internet. Do you believe that Amelia Earhart did not face adversity being the first woman to fly across the Atlantic Ocean? Do you believe that Steve Jobs did not face challenges when creating Apple computers? Of course they suffered, as will you. But on the days when they *didn't feel like it*, they reached down into the depth of the beautiful human spirit, and said, "I will not be beaten." They sacrificed so that others would have more, because that is the reason for our creation.

My son, Noah Abram Still, died so that I could write this book and impact you. His two-day life was his gift to me. With his gift, I now have purpose. Everyday I wake up with a plan to impact the lives of others. Do I feel like it everyday? Well, sure, there are days I'm tired, feeling down, and feeling unmotivated. But what honor or tribute is it to Noah's short life if I do nothing with his memory? You have grappled with tough questions throughout your reading of this book. You have peered into dark crevices and shined a light on places you didn't even know existed. Now I will ask you one final question: with all you have learned, with all you have experienced, with all you have become, what will you do to give the gift of your purpose?

REFLECTION EXERCISE

In what way has this book led you to your own self-discovery?

_____

_____

_____

_____

_____

NOTES

NOTES

Made in the USA
Middletown, DE
24 April 2018